Camille Martin, a Toronto poet and collage artist, is the author of *Codes of Public Sleep* (Toronto: BookThug, 2007). She was born in El Dorado, Arkansas, and spend her childhood in Lafayette, Louisiana. A classical musician from an early age, she earned graduate degrees in both music and English literature. After residing in New Orleans for fourteen years, following Hurricane Katrina in 2005 she moved to Toronto, where she teaches writing and literature at Ryerson University. Her current work-in-progress is a long poem entitled 'The Evangeline Papers,' based on her Cajun/Acadian heritage and drawing on her recent visit to Nova Scotia to participate in an archaeological dig at Beaubassin and to research Acadian and Mik'maq history and culture. Her website is www.camillemartin.ca.

**Also by Camille Martin**

Codes of Public Sleep

# Sonnets

## CAMILLE MARTIN

Shearsman Books
Exeter

Published in the United Kingdom in 2010 by
Shearsman Books Ltd
58 Velwell Road
Exeter EX4 4LD

www.shearsman.com

ISBN 978-1-84861-070-5
First Edition

**Acknowledgements**
I gratefully acknowledge the editors of the following jour-
nals and presses, who published some of the sonnets in this
collection, in some cases in earlier versions:

*5_ Trope, American Letters & Commentary, Angel House Press,
Brown Box, Eleven Eleven, e.ratio, experiment-o, Fell Swoop, Fiera
Lingua, Hamilton Stone Review, Jacket, Literary Review of Cana-
da, moria, Stride, Tammy, This, unarmed, Walrus, West Coast Line,
White Wall Review*

Thanks to Jiří Novak, Jordan Scott and Stuart Ross for their
perceptive and helpful readings of the manuscript.

The author gratefully acknowledges the support of the
Ontario Arts Council.

ONTARIO ARTS COUNCIL
CONSEIL DES ARTS DE L'ONTARIO

Cover: 'Harvest' (collage),
copyright © Camille Martin, 2009

for Jiří

CB

comatose in paradise, but happy, happy
feet! is this where i want to go? thrust
into an age unfavourable to being
a guest in one's own home? the guest
so evolved its dying smile causes
offspring to birth on the spot? progeny
doomed to fail superbly, like houdini's
fetters? is this what i want? am i lucky to think
i am? these twittering birds have nothing
on the silence of magicians from the grave. someday
paradise will be thought savage. did rain fall
because i wanted to write a poem about love,
causing significant damage to blameless paper?
here comes the bus, fool. is that it?

ೞ

i gave you all my sense, blind homunculus,
a sea in a sea. but i'm far from broke.
do you love me, zombie? your main products
are indigo, figments, tricks of cardiac debt,
and a defiant sponge. sometimes your vision,
fluorescent and copious, undershines the diamonds
of your rods and cones and you have to wriggle
your way back, salmon-like, up the information
spillage to the enchanted vapour. you preen
your molecules, all the while scorning the witness
of your deposed gleam. and on your own
little hillside, your own fraudulent
elsewhere, flashing your mirrors into the sun,
you grow roots of endless delay.

಄

like tattered orisons at the end
of a leash, tiny threads of dna flutter
at the bottom of a lake, fragments
betraying the scent of an era, gnomic
figments noticed by none, dispersed
in the murky water breathed by all.
native lumens draft the next
weave, coaxed by drifts of thought
under a sun snoozing off its revels.
a wandering arsonist randomly
sets fire to leaves. moves her hand to write
her lonely fiction. holds her pressure
to the heft. outs her story
for good.

C3

dear incisions: you've amassed a stockpile
of blunders that it was already too late to start
amassing. your fallen muse jars your trance
into a stupor as soon as you start to quench
the gloom of your fragments with a comforting
plot. or maybe not, but there it is, the machine
of your lonely attention constantly initiating shreds
of gratuitous otherness. hazards trapped
in your diced time wail their winged alarms.
and so, dear incisions, enthrall in turn
your testy fool ahead of its grasp. stave in
the hull and shed your muscly garb before
the fossil moon arrives once more
to botch the conning jolt to richer air.

CG

suppose flatness. what then? suppose even surface
is made up. what then? what if i dent itty bitty
identities and remember to smithereens heroic saps
going all the way to town to purchase the certainty
of a certainty, inevitable as a holiday's colours,
sucking along the way for an unconditional bruise,
superior equilibrium undone? lottery glitch. what
then? depending on the deep ending of the handmaiden
to deep identity, the moral of this tale's a little too
complacent, says the sweat of a flea. not enough,
says itinerant dust drifting into a beggar's eyes.
a good enough catalyst comes along once per
flash. no big deal, but here's just enough straw
to make my little nest. what then?

CଽS

**poor souls 1**

you already know how i came home.
i saw a yellow wooden house.
i'm always blundering into difficulties.
the case drags on and on.
and this mood comes over me more and more often.
i finally grow contemptuous of myself.
i must change the ribbon on my hat.
then what would i do with my boots?
i'm afraid something will happen if i go on like this.
it's a tangled affair.
yes, anything may happen.
but the last moments are the worst.
there can be no further discussion of it.
let us finish these ripe plums.

℅

## coma, amok

whatever i think to ask sinks into a coma
and will not surface for air. "what is it?" whispered
naively is my madeleine, and i'm unable
to enter stage right because the prompter has eaten
the little cake that would've clarified everything. whatever
words i write—pub, subway, home—chill
into the numbness of replicas. i'm not
home yet. i'd like to be, but the train keeps
halting, blindly following its route.
whatever i think to do blossoms into
catatonia. the train glides into shifting
terrains. my birthplace recedes into a blank page.
whatever i think to say—casual greeting or rant—
heads home and runs amok.

℃ℨ

i dissipate when you need
me most—what am i?
i dig in when you
most need to be alone
with your regret—what
am i? maybe you won't mind
if i just leave you
clawing the air—what am
i? what if i settle
in for a while, your
worst memory—what am i?
or else i'll morph into
you—but what if there's
no you? what am *i*?

## parroted weeds


i


so many melodies are lost in the time it takes
to sing. to sing is to quote a slice of lore's
flashy highlights. into light's lonely dwelling
is born a blundering fool. the fool's entranced
lion roars a raw, mystic language. in the language
of its brand new country, "honey" means "hamlet."
hamlet is lost in a labyrinth, at the heart of which,
a velvety orange. orange is the fervour of the foreign blue
night. in the night the bees buzz. they buzz and buzz
just as birds know bird things. thing is, you just can't kiss
life the way you used to. i used to rock the boat like i now
court the lapsed muse of dust. dust motes and sky's pressure
are beautiful if not terribly important to them.
they can't get you for that, can they?

ii

if only memory held the key. if traces were the key to grammar
not yet grammar. if the brute sound waves of jackhammers
were a way to witness. the memory of brutes is brutes
remembering or something remembering brutes. cleaving
or cleaving to. typical, like photographs imagining they capture
perfect moods. just perfect, think the photographs
as they capture brute space. they feel limited. if only they had
perfect readers to rescue them, though readers are unreliable
witnesses. they limit, they garble. they cannot rescue all
their moments. at best, they rescue typical
memories of random jackhammers in crowds. at best,
moments emerge and disintegrate, like babbling crowds
at their not-yet grammar. at best, the crowds are random.
if random, then rescue. if rescue, then witness.

iii

**katrina, tundra**

i make up paths that end without warning
in the eye of the storm. i know which path to take,
but once i start thinking, deciding becomes
impossible. on the tundra, old juniper bushes were once
juniper berries. i gaze at the news on tv, old enough
to bury childish nostalgia but not too old to cultivate
obsessive watching. a child in the public library,
i gazed at the yellowing pages of sapphire tundra
lakes. i learn of the yellowish waters
of the flood. i learned that ptarmigans
turn white in winter and gazed at an island afloat
in the middle of water shimmering
in the wintry sun. in my neighbourhood,
islands of red ants float in filthy water.

iv

it is the winter of our maudlin logic. logically,
sadness over spilt clouds includes the drained
colour of snow. crying a puddle
of water, the queen reads the sad story
of her voyage through barren woods. weather
reports expire in yesterday's puddled
footprints. the queen, painting herself
into a corner, instructs her mournful scribe to write
footprints into the plan. scribbling we go, treading
down the wheat. the wheat belongs to the queen,
who banishes us to a land of barren furrows.
our furrowed brows point to winter's
orion, toward which the blue queen sails
on a sea of spilt milk.

v

pomegranate surface beckons. gladly, pomegranates
look to fledglings to cross indigo gulfs. fledglings
fancy cliffs as befits going forth. broken-in paper
under spider chandeliers. spiders weaving seamless
rope unbeknownst. indigo motion streaming
from a transparent nest. unbeknownst, seamless blank
beckons. blank flukes in a kingdom of pure ochre. indigo
and ochre in a blank scape. pomegranates gladly, blank
pomegranate sheen of sculpting light. morning dew settles
on verbal sleep, nothing settled. dusty plain under
wax flock. spiders boarding pretend paper
boats. fabricated gulf crossed by print on folded
cliffs. indigo blanks going forth. verbal
fledglings unbeknownst. unbeknownst.

vi

black asterisk in a black alphabet.
a question of the love of larvae. lovely
birth of larvae in yellow silk or yellow
brass. milky decorum or exo-skeleton
in the metropole. celestial urns and baskets, many
baskets mocking purple robins. why? paper cut
willow blues, willow socket shocks. motifs
appear. again, motifs and a coccyx twin.
sheepish angels in a starry slipcase mingle stone
or stones and blurry angels. a sudden folding,
a sodden book, abruptly sullen. is it signed
by paper prophets? is it numbered? acorns
are new. eels cascade. acorns are sadly news.
o bittersweet, bittersweet black sheep!

vii

footfalls on snow pass other footfalls.
underfoot, furrows crisscross the sleeping
kingdom. over sleep's pages creep gambits.
in the king's gambit, subjects open their books
to the flight of unorthodox birds. the birds announce
the untimely demise of the king. "it was time,"
they chirp, "for winter, and anyway, what's
the matter with bad news? there's cruelty
in the pirouettes of tiniest matter. locks
cruelly breed locks." with that, they flit away
to their otherworldly nests to breed more
discontent in the kingless realm. "there's no *time*
for winter!" cries the king's ghost as he watches
his subjects pass each other in the snow.

viii

glib spice announces the news bleeding
in the monochromatic distance. the short-term
memory of distance flees in fear. enemies
fall, money flees. falling gloom dazzles just
as history taught it to. not the history of stars
made of tumbleweed nor the annals of a dust mote
singing rich disaster. masoch was never so rich,
or so it seems to each geological layer. no
notebook records a pocket of posies between thick
layers of ash. it just is, caught in a small pocket
of time. "it's time to return to star," announces
tumbleweed on the news. the news shrinks
to a speck of pollen on a posy's anther
in a pocket caught between thick layers of ash.

ix

disoriented moths flutter toward quivering red
dwarves. spring's quivering sheen dances
over a meadow's candytufts. scribes afflicted
with dancing plague trace the air in scribbles legible
to their hearts alone. across the sky streaks a molten mass
of gold orchestrating fragile heartbeats. a spill
spreads over gold-flecked formica like a prayer's
nightmare. for the love of awakening
stutters, a hairline crack spreads across an egg.
rooftops tremble in the wake of primordial
night. under roofs, dust praised by none frolics
in heady swirls. some squandering death's head peers
around every corner. peerless lumens orient moths
above the quilt of dusk.

x

addresses harbour night lights glowing
off painted walls. painted ghosts hover over
beds, dreaming of wilderness beyond walls. wild
is the pleasure of unseen treetops scribbling text
into the guiding breeze. the breeze blows letters
under the door. dreaming ghosts read
the letters inside the house, whose coordinates
glide off a map clutched by a visitor lost
in the black night. the visitor stumbles
down the street and into the garden, peering
through windows at ghosts reading letters
by the glow of night lights. what streets lead
to latticed sleep? what silhouettes and fragments
inhabit shades unburdened by light?

xi

jacob's coat of many colours covers
the earth. people sit on the coloured
stripes meditating on the moon.
the moon is stained with the blood
of shape-shifting priests in the form
of bats. the bats collide
with the luminous fossil despite
the tricks of their shifting swarms.
the people crane their necks
to see the spectacle, driven
like a vine searching for a glint
of light. and jacob? jacob's fate
will be decided in the next story,
which recounts the revolt of the moon.

xii

belief stutters from the start.
if you believe in flaming octaves,
you'll be rewarded with flaming
octaves. scandalous tongue-twisters
are their own reward. news
of a scandal takes on an authority
of its own and spreads like a virus.
like old news, vestiges of hollow
metaphors reverberate. the newly
frozen ground translates into
soothing inked paper. i'm so
accustomed to frozen rivulets on rocks
i don't see them anymore.
now i do.

xiii

scenery constantly changes out the window
of the bus. is there constant plunging death
in the blur? the bus rolls along an endless tongue.
my tongue will not wrap around the words
of the next line, so in silence i hear them
bubble to the surface, gather, await
syntax, another kind of death. forever 8:57
on a silent sign. somewhere, pigeons forever
nestle on ledges against the cold. cold syntax
appraises me as my ship sinks. it extends no hand
to save me, but i love it anyway and keep rowing
my lifeboat. all day out the bus's window,
the sun is a constant. it arches across the sky,
oblivious to wax-winged syntax.

xiv

soon the driver will announce the border.
in a borderline whine, the kid behind me says,
"i wanna go home!" cumulonimbus clouds always
remind me of home. crossing borders
is always risky. little pennies risk
being caught rolling across borders. in winter,
little ponds here (and surely also
there) haven't even frozen. now we're even
with the border and its flashing green
and yellow lights—proceed when clear.
it's not clear what country we're in: what's
your licence number need your i.d. how many
on board? now we enter the next country
where everything's full of perfection and fear.

xv

cranes lift junky scraps. slagheaps and scraps
pile up in a car graveyard near shiny yellow
school buses. the parking lot mirrors dim
cars on a pretend pond. dark's one word,
dull's another, though streets glisten
in the dim winter dusk. winter's a dull
boy who stares at the playground but forgets
about recess. sleet streaks a diagonal
across the window of my brain. i borrow
the window between blinks and give it
back, embellished with graffiti. melting
snow gives back accidental scraps. frozen filth
and flying white flurries are both ideal states.
will geese never fly north?

## glasshouse chimes

i

this is the tune that paper sang.
these are the words that graced the tune
that paper sang. this is the loom
that wove the words that graced the tune
that paper sang. this is the flame
that burned the loom that wove the words
that graced the tune that paper sang.
this is the fly that fanned the flame
that burned the loom that wove the words
that graced the tune that paper sang.
this is window that let out the fly
that fanned the flame that burned the loom
that wove the words that graced the tune
that paper sang.

ii

sixpence to feed the flocks
sixpence to drown the rocks
sixpence to crack the eaves
sixpence to climb the stairs
until they end
sixpence to fell the leaves
sixpence to weave a blanket
without a thread
sixpence to dry the wells
sixpence to burn the hearts
in their lairs
sixpence to rock the bells
and hear them knell
until they stop

iii

a room of scribbles and not of harvest
is like a shoreline full of riddles;
and when the riddles begin to sink,
it's like a goldrush full of absence;
and when the absence begins to linger,
it's like a handprint on the ocean;
and when the ocean falls asleep,
it's like a darkness in the marrow;
and when the marrow begins to stammer,
it's like a question through a prism;
and when the prism begins to breathe,
it's like a waltz upon a boat;
and when the boat begins to think,
it's like a scribbler in a room.

iv

if all the seas were one big sea,
then cats would marry poodles.

if baby and i were baked in a pie,
the dog would eat the mop.

if the sun were to shine in the midst of the night,
i'd fly away with a pipe.

if a cat came fiddling out of a barn,
then plums would grow on thistles.

if i built a swine a silver sty,
then herrings would grow in the wood.

if all the food were paving stones,
then swans could swim the sea.

if apples enough were in the barrel,
then little jack could eat.

v

a simpleton inherits a kingdom after unwittingly avoiding
the king's traps of boiling oil and poisonous snakes. he wins the hand
of the lovely princess, who takes her knife out of its sheath,
and seeing blood on the blade, sets about pulling weeds
in the secret garden planted by the late king's gnomes. the simpleton
gives her a box of pears to console her, but the wretched girl searches
in vain for cabbages. she ties a knot in her kerchief and strikes
the ground three times with it, but no wizard appears
to grant her wish. driven mad by remorse, she runs and runs, chasing
mice and repeating: "here come the bird droppings! let us fly away
to the seashore!" finally she travels to a secluded corner of the forest,
where she dies on the bank of a river. near the river is a magnificent
palace where a lovely princess lives with her doting father,
who issues a challenge to all the kingdom's bachelors.

හ

does it take being startled by the ghosts
of a lonely childhood to make a start?
ghosts that feel their way along a rope
dividing the big sea? does the big sea
spawn punctual clouds drifting
toward their little pond? is the little pond
not to be found? does it take releasing
the rope to step conditional steps toward
home, though trackers keep fixing home
to an unreassuring block? does it take
closing one's eyes to see the old street
strung with alphabetical moorings?
does it take unmooring the street?
one's eyes? mute mountains?

୦ଓ

muggy climate: empty signals converse
in calculated jest. in the framed facsimiles
of twisted spawn with awkward gaze,
dendrites with blank agency reach across
the hazy sky. shadows leak from dull objects. wavy
mirages rise from scorching streets like ghostly
mortuaries. sweaty arms evoke the enigma
of the casual acuity of light revealing nothing.

there's you and me in the snapshot, recognizable
if out of focus in translucent space. ears
register the jaded cheer of an ice-cream truck.
here we are giants, see? and here, back to little.
hand waves crisp as the green leaves' burnt edges.
smiles no looser than a doll face carefully spilt.

CB

dark corner, bare bulb, square
one thought. hearth with care-
ful ashes. rocker, unoccupied.
embroidered shrine: marriage's framed
zygotes. cow-eyed portraits.
all-season ancestors,
carpet. everlast bricks
irrelevant. modern kitchen defunct.
growl morphs into rattle. a thimble
of ouch matches brown
accessories. whatever works.
a little string, a little dust.
take a pinch of salt
and measure it.

℃Ʒ

i flaunt remembrance in inky woods, quote
lapses of blue shadows. for all the inevitable
holes in my umbrella, i follow my calling
to a better history. aura off-centre, i have no say
about species or constellations, only homemade
osmotic patchwork and wafts from alien breezes,
the better to witness the sweet comedy
of an unmoored you blowing steepled flecks
into nothing. good, now there's an ongoing you
who performs brilliant arcs in secret
weightlessness. someday we'll form a cult, lowercase
you and i. our notoriety will gallop over fields!
we'll tell ourselves we're happy, even
as we dissolve into the wilderness of my voice.

CB

and if and might within the magic
bowl and bugles native you be
anywhere calmly flying whole
upon a supper of leaves and pearl
where written lands run red to break
the method of the next bright place
on rooftops' tasted air and colour
with somehow miracle you yourself
to please the careless holiday
with gifts of blended orbits sung
in knee-deep bubbling seconds listening
at the end to stay the now
to start this famous morning with its
flooded velvet baby navel cell

cs

start-
ing from one breath and
a sharp loc-
us, unwitting choices
spew chaotic
albeit genuine sp-
ume and in that
bedlam levees over-
flow and lost words plash
onto feral shoals, syn-
tax prematurely ashore
and wound up, tense
as the one that got a-
way

CR

i would have swum to you, knowing how
flames could billow and languish, their surviving
luminosity melting colours off burnished leaves.
or this: a ribbon unwinds the heady scent of one
unsolved riddle to the next. wheels careen along
the undulating strip toward a city of shimmery
sounds trickling down to fill eggshells. vandals
emblazon the stars from their rickety balconies.
 i can see the reckless mammals vividly, splashing
violet onto blue, protoplasm onto zeppelins. nesting
as i do in the superstitious relic of my past, nonetheless
i saved eons for your cerulean arrival. of course
it *would* turn out that i could write about it
only by *not* writing about it.

CB

i said i was happy, but that
was an interpretation.
the wide-eyed bride runs out of
time zones and into wheels
of daily attention thinking
false green thoughts
dancing for rain beneath
patchy clouds, all the while
loathing elements, *the*
elements, on transient
principle, and pleasuring half–
blind rules governing un–
controllable names:
an interpretation of happy.

ೞ

if i should cancel the allegories i love. if instincts
should recoil into birdlike facts. if staves
of indecipherable music should offer
a legend of leitmotifs in a tonic key. if i should mistake
volume for life, lost in an arcadian forest. if i should lose
my wishes, wild kite tails later, to schooled airstreams.
if i should dive into pedigreed lakes yielding their fields
of wrinkled proofs. if i should cross the "t" of she but mean
a surprised "i." if i should mix blithe hours with the ashes
of pantocratic frowns. if i should trust the messages of smiling
weather reports, oblivious to the murmurs of chatting
wisps of wind. if i should forget feigned
analogies rioting on their axes. if i should abandon
toy boats whirring on living seas.

ℭ

someday i'll find myself like a phantom
of patched-up winter, clumsy in the stuttering
clutter, succumbing to currents of silence,
unable to perceive latent fruits in a forest
with no observer. is there no other way
to the ground but a sideways breath rushing over
my shoulder to the rightness of nothing, clock-a-clay?
blizzards digress as i strain to catch a hint
of music and prophets mumbling
their readings of trellised sand. i've come to an end
of bare trees and their ever-splitting branches
networking the big slate. the mesh finally
shatters the coldness into a sapphire junkheap
as looping signals fade.

෪

red balls bounce up the street,
splashing in the lavish rain.
they are propelled by the thoughts
of acrobats breathing orange ether,
ovalesque rhythm spreading
to their legs and arms. mechanical
crickets in the purplish dawn sprinkle
their chirrups onto the street, feeding
crops of children's hands that sprout
along the sidewalk. the hands
break loose from their stems.
they are the swing shift.
they take over as bouncing red balls
retire to their slumber.

**catastrophe theory**

i

mammals and crickets breathe tomorrow's
weather. matter-of-factly they sip their tea and absorb
its little catastrophes with the calmness of a cloudy
dawn observed through a clear window. slowly, glass panes
weep for blooms and scorched blooms, oaths broken
and kept. waves vanish into glitter while empty cups
loom. tomorrow, that is. better yet, whatever angle lurks
curves dash. on an afternoon just like this one,
is the title of a book, a real page-turner ending
with a cliff-hanger: a tightrope walker takes a deep breath
and bravely steps onto his fleeting wire. he can still feel
the breeze, and for him, too, tomorrow's weather never
dies. so he vows to balance, stick perpendicular
to the wire, and matter-of-factly turns the page.

ii

spring's blind surge awakens rambling epics. evidence
gushes. first things jockey for position. feet sink
into mud, and revelation looms at the cost of sleep. even
a car sounds different. the exotic bark of a dog shatters
orion, spilling sand from a stunned hourglass.
thereafter, molecules relax and history tries again:
a garlanded mother emerges playing a kithara
as her darlings weave a pedestal, the better to adore
the quixotic colourist: proof that sensory deprivation
binds minions to a redundant deity. lids can't filter
catastrophic light. sap's flight quickens, guiding
moments trickling toward a slack horizon. and again:
over the years weep scullions at their skinned rabbits.
peddlers of risk lean into showers of delinquent buds.

iii

twigs with tiny
variations bob
against the blue.
no gunshot, no
sprint. earth murmurs
on its axis, volume turned
off. no hearts beating
to drums. seeds hook
animal fur. no countdown,
but a desert blossoming
between one and zero.
droplets fed by tiny
catastrophes dangle
from twigs.

iv

dear heady dogma, i've always loved your daily
bells and shiny apples, the sophistry of your symbol:
a frozen planet in a child's colouring book. your memory
of a movie still is like a movie still. or like being
in a train rushing through a tunnel, snapshots
of lights gliding along the black walls, glass
overlaid with a steady veneer of interior. dear lowly
magma, you murmur of the sparks flying from images
in the catastrophic night. in your ocean,
each kind meets green thoughts fattened by blood
vessels. in the end, empty miasma, you offer
gifts of brilliant lemons and little snails, a tale clad
in simple red, calico dusk, blue of sailing winds, as if
they had any say in the matter.

v

a word is lost.
ruddy-cheeked cherubs flutter up a filament
rising from the centre of a compass. weather systems
with their odious troughs and frontal depressions
shape continents. not lost its way.
vanished. heaven is supposedly at the end
of the thread. one raindrop more finds its puddle,
or less, isn't missed by moths. one word less
to describe the precise iridescence of their wings.
the filament was imagined and so were the cherubs.
one trifling subtraction and the keystone evaporates.
catastrophic detour. heaven's architecture
crumbles. no limitless blue skies,
but a tempest, lost.

**on merest sand**


i.


the levee of the mississippi, high
as a mountain ridge. the path, slippery, laced
with puddles. how small, human-sized
the vast river seems from this vantage point.
how ironic it'd be, drowning in a puddle imagining
the undertow of the mississippi. the levee
slopes down closer to the banks. i'm astonished
to see kittens delicately leaping onto the river
and padding with dry paws on diaphanous sheets
thrown onto the rippling current. mysterious
hands gently flap the sheets over the water and float
them for the kittens, hoards of them now
arriving at the shore, deftly bounding
onto the cloth spread by unknown hands.

ii.

from a helicopter at night, an aerial
view of a city. in the dark, gigantic
iron statues loom with an ominous
aura of permanence. the people
who live in the city obsess
about the possibility of doomsday
erupting among their soaring
buildings and effigies. of the end
they've made a fetish, chatting
about it at cocktail parties as if
it were the latest vogue. they believe
that it could happen at any
moment, so they no longer bother
to make their beds in the morning.

iii.

i release the spirit of my puritan
ancestor, who recites a poem
about the ringing of silver bells
at the funeral of a mail carrier.
i tell him i think the poem
ironic, believing it spoke to a fumbling
of nerve deep in the holds
of the first vessels to heave anti-
matter onto wild shores. to him,
the poem is serious, pious,
deserving of recitation to a more worthy
audience. i smile to myself. he says,
"you have a smile like a frog."
this pleases me enormously.

⍣

the            sun was enamoured of the
concept        that most, if not all,
of             the apples of the world have a sweet
meaning.       "i'll lower my bucket," said the sun, "which
is             vast enough to hold the ruddiest apple of
every          apple tree beneath my path." the sun
bit            into the first apple it saw as soon
as             the bucket returned. but the apple's meaning proved
problematic    for the sun. its rays turned the apple, as red
as             the reddest sunset, into ashes whose significance
the            sun was unable to fathom. in fact, the very
concept        of the meaning
of             the once-rosy apple eluded the overheated
mind           of the sun, consumed as it was by the problem.

54

CB

before painted fruit and flowers, nothing survived.
dinosaur tracks evolve in the wandering cognition
of wingless creatures. sadness about elusive treasure seeks
a colossal crane. my ship has sailed and is gone forever.

phantom storms capsize phantom ships. cold
latitudes of blindness orbit consciousness.
sleep scribbles latent flora, effacing genuine
blooms. a being signals and errs forever.

rainy wind, drained of depth but still its own
cosmos of doubtful gestures. impossible to stay
in one place—the mind would vanish. across the sky
cottony mammals parade, shifting forever.

vaguely happy people march into their shelters.
a doll awakens to life, becomes a toy forever.

ભ

dusk of airless balloons floating stems-down to pitched slab

•

dusk of heaven's puzzled kiss athwart shifting rooftops

•

dusk grows, lighting speechless verbs perched on dim cattle

•

shiny eggs toned down by dusk on the edge of a cottoned gong

•

dusky fossil sonata rippling toward impoverished fringes

•

scarcely swarming dusk in soft paralysis

•

dusk of tomorrow's noon, dissolving in past imperfect vats

•

hairline cracks in unwitting dusk emitting ceaseless whiles

•

dusk of rhythmic erasure, shielded waifs, recoiling flags

•

one hand reaching one dusk, tumbling looser seasons

•

dusk threshing dust in zero gravity for evasive retinas

•

rich dusk plunders photons muted in the burgeoning blur

•

dusk in turn envelops the blind buzz of sifted bells

•

dusk of unknown mollusks awash in the honing dusk

ଓ

i wish i could write on all the sand in the world.
history books narrate centuries of dust and revenue.
punching keys, i still call it scribbling.
writing scratches the surface of paper.
my pretend twin reads a book of empty water.
walking along a path, i carried a newsy letter.
and on the way i lost it.

i fear to read the words on a small windowpane.
in a plotless hush, now becomes bankrupt and void.
asking soothing questions, i unname the clean page.
reading digs a bottomless abyss.
my true self dreams a sea of hollow letters.
dashing through wastelands, i lost my spurious myth.
and going back i found it.

ભ

**poor souls 2**

i copied it out of some book.
what a kind heart you have, do lend me something.
i decided to read it, as quickly as possible.
what's the use of writing this?
i've never read a better book in all my life.
you say that you are useless?
there are many of them, all rare and expensive.
they are starving.
i should read it again with attention.
now, i must say a few words.
but enough of this.
we really don't need so much.
it's all talk and nothing else.
i know nothing and have read nothing.

&#x43;&#x297;

all day, innocent nebulae travel,
outstripping clay animals preening
their quivering ideas, tipped in gold.


•


an apothecary shifts golden
abacus beads to the left and right,
as if positions were the matter.


•


every time the prince reaches toward
the singing ruby apple with golden
stem, the song of the apple recedes.


•


an impossible moon lowers its gilded horns
and charges the flux and babble
of everything from iron to meat.


•


onto the wizard chanting a spell to restore
confidence in spells, fool's gold rains.

ᚳᚷ

## noathon

thought defeats its own grasp
and is in turn routed by its fake
signature. it is a trembling blot
infected with significance,
a gluttonous burlesque of absence
within its hermitage. its tongue
ad-libs counterfeit text
and calls the indefinite home.
it observes the arc of its decay
and blurs its careful schemes
with plodding squalls, countermands
the awful simplicities entering the eyes.
its here is not here.
it has resolutely gone into an other.

ᘓ

i'd like to help your famously habitual 71% water,
i really would. i'd like to unmake the myth of you,
render your pronounceable mouth unintelligible, whisper
into your kosher rods and cones rumours of universal
blindness. i'd love to introduce your contortionist amigdala
to a slacker dawn, overflow your schooled love
with melismatic phonemes, your stitched-up largest organ
circumambulating without a stitch. in short,
to disturb your utopian house, place your clandestine
freak front and centre, spouting cl-cl-classics of slangy
topoi. but then again, i enjoy too much building
the little structure of you and then blowing it up, prompting
the grinds to discover epic lines between the stars
of your infidel constellations.

୯ଌ

however you endeavour to sever the found
ground or ring of things too soon to be a boon
to a tablespoon of sable moon, or whenever
you forget to fret over being so uncool as to drool
like a thread from a spool to foolishly eat
the sweet bread of love above the foxgloves that dwell
in the spell of blood-red flood, or wherever you table
the middle of riddles or fiddle with the pith of a fable
of a dove's farewell to flat eggshells that scatter
all the rules of scrawl, you risk landfall, after which,
whisked away, straightaway you sway to the call
of nightfall's fireball and pray with an ache and a pang
to forsake the break and the tall harangue of day
to recall the plight and twang of splaying flight.

∞

grateful readers wish
for complicit acrobats, the whole
showy boom with harboured
context and bowered skin, flowers
urging factories to crumble
under winds that come and go.
i overflow in useless, bereft
years, deteriorating gurgles.
my bedevilment stone says
to feed my flow with devious
dust and paint illusive shadows.
again and again i erode
origins in the dim haven
of my one slight eye.

**reft link**

crown crown crown crown crown crown crown crown
crown crown crown crown crown crown crown crown
crown crown crown crown crown crown crown crown
crown crown crown crown crown crown crown crown
crown crown crown crown crown crown crown crown
crown crown crown crown crown crown crown crown
crown crown crown crown crown crown crown crown
crown crown crown crown crown crown crown crown
crown crown crown crown crown crown crown crown
crown crown crown crown crown crown crown crown
crown crown clown crown crown crown crown crown
crown crown crown crown crown crown crown crown
crown crown crown crown crown crown crown crown
crown crown crown crown crown crown crown crown

frame frame frame frame frame frame frame frame
frame frame frame frame frame frame frame frame
frame flame frame frame frame frame frame frame
frame frame frame frame frame frame frame frame
frame frame frame frame frame frame frame frame
frame frame frame frame frame frame frame frame
frame frame frame frame frame frame frame frame
frame frame frame frame frame frame frame frame
frame frame frame frame frame frame frame frame
frame frame frame frame frame frame frame frame
frame frame frame frame frame frame frame frame
frame frame frame frame frame frame frame frame
frame frame frame frame frame frame frame frame
frame frame frame frame frame frame frame frame

brink brink brink brink brink brink brink brink
brink brink brink brink brink brink brink brink
brink brink brink brink brink brink brink brink
brink brink brink brink brink brink brink brink
brink brink brink brink brink brink brink brink
brink brink brink brink brink brink brink brink
brink brink brink brink brink brink brink brink
brink brink brink brink brink brink brink brink
brink brink brink brink brink brink brink brink
brink brink brink brink brink brink brink brink
brink brink brink brink brink brink brink brink
brink brink brink brink brink blink brink brink
brink brink brink brink brink brink brink brink
brink brink brink brink brink brink brink brink

flee flee flee flee flee flee flee flee flee
flee flee flee flee flee flee flee flee flee
flee flee flee flee flee flee free flee flee
flee flee flee flee flee flee flee flee flee
flee flee flee flee flee flee flee flee flee
flee flee flee flee flee flee flee flee flee
flee flee flee flee flee flee flee flee flee
flee flee flee flee flee flee flee flee flee
flee flee flee flee flee flee flee flee flee
flee flee flee flee flee flee flee flee flee
flee flee flee flee flee flee flee flee flee
flee flee flee flee flee flee flee flee flee
flee flee flee flee flee flee flee flee flee
flee flee flee flee flee flee flee flee flee

prow prow prow prow prow prow prow prow
prow prow prow prow prow prow prow prow
prow prow prow prow prow prow prow prow
prow prow prow prow prow prow prow prow
prow prow prow prow prow prow prow prow
prow prow prow prow prow prow prow prow
prow prow prow prow prow prow prow prow
prow prow prow prow prow prow prow prow
prow prow prow prow prow prow prow prow
prow prow prow prow prow prow prow prow
prow prow plow prow prow prow prow prow
prow prow prow prow prow prow prow prow
prow prow prow prow prow prow prow prow
prow prow prow prow prow prow prow prow

## tellurium candies

i.

wrecked sense beats its curved gong
in the present indicative, leaving behind
snarls of ripples to be pronounced by
other, more omnivorous exegetes.
being largely oblivious, it is also
ungrateful for the palatial labyrinth
of its home in which flame equals
banished flame. glissandi of yeses and nos
echo in the empty hall, deathless toggles
that no puppet master can kill off
to create a more compliant illusion.
broken crowd or broken cloud:
the edges of meek solidity fritter
into the reaches of angel space.

ii

peaceable leeches (who's to say)
seek flaws in the plump
exoticism of one's thirst, dwarf
the livid mortar of one's (dubiously)
intentional totem. what remains
to duly plumb short-term
dazzle reflex or sculpt one's
willowy umbra are these augured
non-sequitur tableaux. wizened
cynic with untold person calls it
a night, even though, cleaving (to)
an essential memory of orangeabilia,
one's marrow twin calls it
a nocturnal spell.

iii

what one hears in the inveterate
"and" is a drowned blueprint, mind
gap or stopgap end-in-sight,
all examples artificial: tiger snarl
fur, gang plank hurtling dumb-
foundedness. garnishers of
plummet survival tales pummel
dedicated corpuscles unfavoured
by fetal ghosts, according to one's
telltale breathing. it's either
ether or ore, according to one's
dainty elephantine vigil praxis.
so leap over the gaps,
sharpshooter target.

iv

plotting unawares the direction of impulse
(which is to say, not plotting at all).
on the verge of pronouncing a shabby
but proud apostrophe. exploiting
bogus entropy to veer off the path wholly
engaged in blended lies and woven
tales. freebasing fiction, hard up
as a blindfolded gambler. desiring
against all the evidence to be duped again
by blinkering syllables as plain as
a bunch of sunflowers peering
through village fog. declaiming a reckless
arabesque to patch up severed
nerve endings with dumb surds.

v

bulging magma gathers
mud, pries fossils aloft, absorbs
chimney spew whose arbitrary
particles merge with the unstoppable.
dappled deeps forge apples
from zip. tomorrow
takes as gospel
scraps of riddles and broken
kinship urging loopy
script. dust skitters in the dawn
of a raggedy broom freewill's
occupied with. flimsy
dust and flimsy dustpan
gladhand. why not?

CB

i've been far too literal. so what will it take
for you to hold out for a rickety machine drowning
in white noise, transposing the pleasure of majestic arcs
into the key of motes? to buy into a futile game
so you can enjoy the half light playing on the lawn
over your half-empty grave? perhaps you've been too sly
for epochs blooming in the sprig of a comma,
for sleepwalkers colonizing a semi-public landscape. perhaps
you've been too absorbed collecting frames to notice
consciousness capsized in purgatory. nonetheless, matter
pronounces victory for its blunder of choice:
"if ever background errors fade from happy frescos, i
and my vibrating airwaves will humbly take leave."
and now for the figurative version.

છ્ક

## poor souls 3

in the sea swim fishes.
if only you could see them.
it's a quarter to three.
the clock has no hands.
the first moment of doubt:
what are you saying?
how should i answer?
all is how it should be.
birds peep. lungs fill.
eggs break. mills grind.
time presses. maybe
this is a love poem.
we are not yet beaten.
there is no other guarantee.

i drink to dreams with spurious punch
on the speck of a map imagining its own
city whose bricklayers wield regrettable
clarity. from the runes on my palms, i recite
a fake history of letters during the endless
recess after stumbling through latin.
when salt air falls in love with the old
school, they call it even steven, even
when tragedy befalls a cobbled-up embryo
and its blasphemes of cynicism from the gitgo.
i am inexplicably late for my lesson on delayed
bewilderment. the story of my bogus playground:
an invisible sail blown by cobalt wind.
a beggar of scarcity just before ample sleep.

ങ

into geography creeps a straw body,
a corpse with mental limbs meandering
in fictive suspense, probing the sky
with its tentative snout. from his perch, the man
in the moon sings to the body songs
of fading dye and threadless looms.
he croons a parable in which embodiment
ends, landscape begins: a rebus without
subject. the body weaves its faulty
plots from the aria's thin air. despite
the zeal of the fossil's tale, the fabric
evaporates each time the man in the moon
tries to read the body's chronicles
in the blush of dawn.

Cʒ

one lucky machine greets another
at the delicate blur of a map's edge. dust
storms whirl entropy across imaginary
borders, a pandemonium more fleeting
than any epiphantic strategy. impostors
with street cred forever harvest
ephemera. every moment, hypotheses
in which to cast hooks. flies fixed
in amber buzz complicity with a chorus
of sleepwalkers droning flimsy
notions before the dwellings of brutes.
disharmony flutters in the airlessness
above encroaching glaciers. useless pennies
twirl on the brink of pointless curbs.

ℭ

what if, in the ragtag season of happy photons
wasting the sky, the last conscious imago,
a crude figure utterly finished as only a loose end
can be, what if it were to unmoor the final instant
from its graffiti? what if, despite the malice
of maps and their pastel patches squandering
cardinal points that float toward oceans like
arrowheads in a stream, what if the shadow
of an insect, an accidental nothing flitting
from its instant were to shatter the sun?
how tangible, how dusk, how melt, how
flash false ethers full of swarms of neutral
beings above the sky, under the earth.
how loose embers might yet loom.

Ↄ

snow.
repeat. flesh
of snow, pocks
in tarnished snow.
snow of lust.
snow of cash.
blathering omega's
travesty of dust.
snow breaking
vows of poverty
but not silence.
snow of theft.
sparrows buried
in snow.

൪

cold windows quietly hoard iridescent ova, i write,
to begin at the brink of something that seems almost
attainable. the prospect looms distantly in cool
meditation, not about to teeter into the first
warm breath to come down the pike and call it
home. i've eaten the last morsel and become a stranger
to myself, as far away as orion wheeling slowly
across the sky. plate empty, i dance to conjure
melted brook as the unmoved sun massively
shrugs off the confabulation of my phantom
gestures. i'm already hungry for the freshly eaten feast,
but even this early in the game, i feel i must deceive
myself as once again synapses conspire to blurt out
a raucous draft of blooms.

CB

and if the seeds and if they sprout in the bulldozed
forest the forest where trees tall and green once
where they once where they swayed in the wind where
treetops back and forth where they waved and if the birds
drop seeds if they drop them on the razed on the vanished
woods where birds remember perches where bird nests
once perched if birds remember if they know that here
they once flew if birds drop to the bare ground if they drop
seeds if the seeds sprout in the mind of the bird if
the bird's mind sprouts if it grows its own perch if that perch
on the sprout in the mind of the bird if the bird's mind remembers
a nest if the eggs in that nest if they hatch if they remember
hatching little birds if the little birds fly over the forest over
the bulldozed forest if they drop seeds and if the seeds

CB

i plant a tree but later i can't find it.
massless light won't quite slant.
rain later proves conceptually wrong.
zombies devour worthless blobs of ink.
stoic electrons ignore stage directions.
lovely petals wear pernicious masks.
so what if it doesn't work, so what?

i welcome flocks of dreams through flimsy doors.
fluted winds rifle moth wings.
lightwaves perpetually beckon windowpanes.
bruised suns twirl in shimmering futility.
sprouting feathers, vagrant gods compete.
spiders drifting homeward paint their webs.
so what if it works, so what?

‰

elsewheres weave joy tents for whales with self-
made frills on, wake stone geese to sharp
heartbeats of their own lost kind, seize air thick
with still-fresh daybreak wrapped in clouds' pale
cloth. elsewhere, nightmare's bloomed shock loves
raindrops' dive-bombed landscape, loves all elsewhere
can rouse drugged skies, heave brave howls
from the once-mute locked maw of one's deep light.
green magpies fly far-off, seek more elsewhere, more
depth where a seahorse with tear ducts weeps in swells
of thick waves, where deft aircraft skim gold
off plump words, where lungs breathe elsewhere's
thoughts, soft ruins where tins strewn pell-mell dream
shell's beast, ring sun's bells, shell one's husk.

ॐ

in beckoning weather they search for ancient wildflowers.

ribboned caresses discover a bed of leaves.

limbs arch at vespers erasing shores.

each interval between motions, superfluous song.

each moment, chronicles of ocean and ocean's twin.

each gaze, portraits in a locket worn by a ghost sailing from thought.

they chase rich flames through lucid air.

black suns dissolve in their brains as a relic glows across a blank slate.

dreams of breaths land gently on horizons and vanish.

under embryonic eyelids, images of dew glistening on brambles.

their veil shielding sunrise belongs equally to the rising sun.

a warbling "maybe" fools trusting ears.

the atmosphere spies their awakening lament.

within a tangled nocturne dwells their slipping away.

ଔ

the view from a hollow
cube—holes covered by clear
liquid sheets ever so
slowly flowing downward,
behind one of which
a recluse observes
the stillness of tiny
birds landing on
ice, pecking at crumbs,
scattering at some
unheard signal that surely
quickens their even tinier
hearts—visible, even so,
through bare twigs and blinds.

൫

the sky above horizon's rim fills with jostling
photons. light circulates around raised
brows, flexible mouths, ambiguous contours.
our shadows lie in veneers of puddles that slip
relentlessly into rivers, leaving us drained
of evidence as we chatter one non sequitur
after another. what about the embassy? proof
will take too long, and they will keep parts
of us in their soft inner lining. our bodies
restively shift like the continental drift, our every
moment a dissonant snapshot superimposed
on stillness. our images always leave
things out, things that bloom in waste places,
winking and nodding.

႙

the minute eyespot of invertebrates, as massive
as an electron, as volatile as the minute eyespot
of invertebrates. membership in the guild of earth
substance causes well-developed but perpetually
outmoded wings to burgeon, based on shapes divined
without recalling the exact chemistry of the waters
from which they sprang. the wings fly to abandoned places
where the minute eyespot of invertebrates emerges
like the mirage of a fabled marine creature on the *qui vive*
for the fragile membrane of prey that also covets
the minute eyespot of invertebrates. the creatures
unwittingly cross the eyespot with raw data, a game
designed for the destruction of all safe havens.
the possible spoils are vast.

CB

**citizen**

in the meagre theatre
of my unfuelled labour,
in the dishonourable parlour
of my moulded behaviour,
marvelling neighbours humour
the rancour and clamour
of my sulphurous demeanour as i,
in the glamour and calibre
of my grey woollen fibre,
in the harbour of my ill-counselled
candour and manoeuvres,
savour my favourite colour
at the unravelled centre
of my vapourish endeavours.

**the street names of toronto**

i.

a great benefactor, you planted more fruit trees
in the aftermath of your tragic death than during
your expansive life. you discovered gold
and had music piped in. and then your name lost an "e"
in a fencing accident. in 1927 you opened the university
of the difficulties of the poor, who danced
a minuet of sublimation rather than eat their soggy
sustenance. armed with pitchforks and other farm implements,
a feed mill and an amusement park managed to survive
your last act as lieutenant governor. we seek you,
great benefactor. although you can still be spotted underwater
or strolling through hollows, you are an unsuitable
subject for the queen. the hurons killed and ate you,
and now you are a street.

ii.

you were a brewer and a faithful methodist. prejudiced
against trees, you imported some of your prize bushes
from a brickyard in scotland. though considered ineffective,
you dreamed of living in a real castle
with thirty bathrooms and ornamental lakes
for the ponies. during the rosedale croquet riots,
the house of lords burned your effigy
at their clubhouse. after hanging the rebels,
you rebuilt your tavern and outlived all your accusers.
eventually your debts drove you to selling candy floss
in public dance halls and lunatic asylums. you left
instructions for your heart to be tucked away
in a place with no alcoholic beverages,
and now you are a street.

iii.

you had the checkered early history
of an anointed bishop who ate french fries
in paper cones and snowflake donuts
on the side. you traded blankets for fishhooks
and carried people, mail, and goods to rousing
camp meetings, despite a good deal of ill feeling.
after you sold most of your land, your name
was often misspelled. in spite of your emotionally
disturbed outlook, you moved to york
at 600 feet per hour and set up a shop that will soon
be razed. in a streak of good fortune, you were knighted
for introducing showgirls and rhubarb to the area.
then dynamite exploded in your face,
and now you are a street.

ଓ

the rug of day. a static bird cleaves
the air, leaving a fleeting memory
of nubs on the ground. morning pastels
suck the wind still. tiny pebbles in a puddle
under a banana tree loosely recollect
concentric ripples. the earth's core listens
to the slow trailing of a snail. at 2:37
in the afternoon, the banana leaves are translucent,
ragged, motionless. a woman strolls past
faces hidden behind blinds, glances at a rigid
centipede on a cracked sidewalk. limpid
air fades. celestial bodies begin directing
the orchestra of crepuscular insects. someone
strums fingertips against a windowsill.

෬

inevitable roofs with antennae. belief's flames
lick the walls while burning curtains billow
toward apocalyptic roads planted with puddles
of liquefied myrrh. god plugged the leaky ceiling
of the sky with noah's animals and that is why
they look down at dry earth with innocent
sadness through an atmosphere thick with certainty.
at a cul-de-sac clogged with weeds, an idea
of perfection, like caravans stopping,
men and women squinting to read the map
on the charred clapboard, then looking
ahead into a valley of swirling climates, tiny
upside-down images of ancient murals
inside their blazing eyes.

CB

the past is inexperienced, but it is the flower
of translation. it returns to a scandal unforeseen
flipping through fate in an almanac. the past
does not correspond to a fall or a harbour. it is not
something to be erased or placed
in an envelope. the past is a pleasure trip
with loss. it questions the words
of a vagabond on a metaphorical bridge.
a document is not the event. it declares
its own film beyond its molecules' tapestry
of stains. the past moults its body with every haphazard
photon, wracks its flair for home. somewhere, icy
gardens recall their tropical prime, and snow
blossoms, divining colder fronts.

෴

a cardboard cutout croons down brazen streets, flustering
the delicate ligaments of january. cheerful but fictitious
confetti drift down from who-knows-where. the resolute
gestures of the adoring crowd fritter into mere traces.
if only they could slacken old habits, they think, they could see
with dry café eyes the white of an orange peel by the light
of doomed planets, erase cardinal points no longer vital
to legendary panoramas, drain from their habitat
brackish day and wasted night. if only they could belt out
their own slow-witted song, carving ruts into blank brains.
perhaps a song about bricklayers who eat oranges and toss
the peels onto brazen streets with counterfeit crooners.
maybe then summer snow would come out of hiding
and latent flowers quiver in their eyes.

ʚ

snow crosses all borders. can you will it
to fall on the feast of the czar? plums
and avocados rot in anticipation
of colours morphing in the blustery wind.
fermentation under the powdery white
blanket passes all understanding despite
intricate synapses sparking around
the table. all this white! why not
orange? the czar with his stained
bib remembers fondly the spheres
of his tender belches amid snow
blown all the way from persia under
the orangey stars he cannot see.
can you?

Cʒ

struggling to make the wind turn the wind-
mill's blades to grind golden outcome: a competent
yield that might purchase bullets to shoot into
a nearby house lined with grimy windows
whose shattering forfeits the obscured view of whatever
pisses, whatever casts tell-tale shadows,
whatever might gaze on broken panes never
again to reflect feathers of thoughts of feathers.
the blades might even rotate, producing
fungible piles of grain, or maybe useless grains
of sand: pointless grinding. then a confused
fall into bramble. rambling failure. in point
of fact, rushing to it through fluid wind,
opening eyes to the oscillations of a fan.

☙

it's winter in a haiku that no one
believes, though its chill survives within all
other seasons. debris from its echoes lies
at the bottom of a cliff, where a woman and a man
with small mouths and wrinkled faces look up
into the freezing air, see each snowflake vanish
on contact. they do not think of copernicus
or astrology or anything between the pages
of a book. migratory birds fly over them
and nothing happens. they stand
on the footprints of jesters who once danced
in a garden, now a silent scree. still
the woman and the man, stooped over, peer
into the cold sky, and nothing seems to happen.

C<sub></sub>හ

fields and lakes and fields
again. just enough
light to see glyphs
scribbled by the tremor
of the highest branch
of a tree. from that branch,
raindrops spattered
onto yesterday's roof. today,
one drip winds up wiped
off a table under still-wet
shingles. up the road,
villages linked by every
curve's tiny house, one
as inevitable as the next.

CЗ

her green sweater, caught in a revolving
door that reflects clouds frittering away
like flour blown off a wooden cutting
board. she looks back. she has no
shadow. thoughts of the shortness
of ant seasons, and whether omens will ever
mean what they mean before coming true.
her eyes, transparent holes in the sky.
light fades into a dusk riddled
with dim constellations and vanishes
into their unconnected dots,
like knots in a magician's scarf.
the key to unhooking her sweater
is a tangled up, long, long time.

**jetsam archive**

i

still at funnel wake,
braided unction stomachs no
crime, spurs no spit of plowed
habit. so, wrong torque? other-
wise puppet? shrieks drain cloistered
moot of leftover ham-fisted
squirm. frail threads ascend
breakage flank, crucified
squander. shift regalia
collapse to lapsed impetus: if decay
veto "as if to say." as if to beg
brawn of pander flint, lucid
hunger spectacle. as if
to bugger lawn.

ii

remember to wind up sockets
to stave off icy clack, yank down
goods that fatten innuendo,
confound eavesdropping bylaws in fluent
mesh, cauterize or maybe ravage folly
(a personalized lilac tomb)
    remember to misapprehend stolen
premises of the demimonde, slice
time in half to strip consoling
brackets, scalp mindless peaks
atop shallows of rank muscle
while trembling before mutant
weeds, haunt the shucked
spinal column once and for all

iii

flinty skin slaps quick fix
on public eye targeting chromatic
plenum: astral scattering
of plumes, crayolas melted
on basalt midnight. exiled
ghost inks reckless glyphs depicting
one penultimate scam or other,
sharpens fetishes in frost-free
outer space. swords deftly sever
links between glittery saint and mock-stone
shrine. likely tickers ponder focal
points of punctured wrecks.
dervishes breach their zeal, twirl
the feverish dust.

iv

enter mirage wink.
splintered questions bray
under exit wreath under jagged grip.
hundred blossom dirt dreams in coffin
façades under liquid rock razing crowded
nothing. so now subjects pelt
crumbly table rubric: staccato epics
to split the code of moldy sheaf,
pellets to wrack slab's raw freak.
fuck agency! that road blackout
between civic snout and halo fire! that
poison picture combing final wave
debris so bullet's whim can better reach.
and now it's time to

v

      and lastly, zither
slash—memorable -copia
for herbaceous calendar fork-
over    what stalled bids a-
ghast one's acumen doggedly
slew   from exquisite morph
to extraneous bastion, false
comet slangily zeroes in on ac-
curacy: cricket xyz (no -fluence)
for 19-gasket formula    cow-
town flap is all the thistle do
jar's about    analogical skin
to contortionist redux—
      a vastly dither mash

ঙ

night wings in the blind atmosphere
sprinkle the ground with dust. you are
your own muscular witness in a way
station of wandering plot. a sprinting
sphinx escorts you, honey milk animal
nothing, to a missing manifold. scribes
croon non-copernican rubatos of carnal doubt
trapped in the sticky fluorescence of bird mango.
you release your most seductive words
into an unfamiliar house of cards. ready?
3-2-1. you are now entering your foreign
birthplace. the sphinx is your guide.
take this placebo and repeat
after the cagey beast:

LaVergne, TN USA
01 April 2011
222583LV00001B/26/P